WATER GARDENING

PHILIP SWINDELLS

HarperCollinsPublishers

Products mentioned in this book

'Clean-Up' contains tar acids

'*Clean-Up*' is a trade mark of Imperial Chemical Industries plc
Read the label before you buy: use pesticides safely.

Editor Maggie Daykin
Designers James Marks, Steve Wilson
Picture research Moira McIlroy

First published 1988 by
HarperCollins Publishers

This edition published 1992

A CIP catalogue record for this book is available from the British Library.

Photoset by Bookworm Typesetting
Printed and bound in Hong Kong by Dai Nippon Printing Company

Front cover: Nymphaea 'Escarboucle'
Back cover: Garden pool
Both photographs by The Harry Smith Horticultural Photographic Collection

CONTENTS

Introduction	**4**
Siting the Pool	**6**
Pool Design	**8**
Pool Construction	**10**
Fountains and Waterfalls	**16**
Planting the Pool	**20**
Plant Propagation	**26**
Stocking with Animal Life	**28**
Pond Problems	**33**
Pests and Diseases	**35**
Gardening Year	**36**
Sixty of the Best	**38**
Index and Acknowledgements	**48**

INTRODUCTION

Water gardening is a fascinating hobby that can be enjoyed at any age. And water adds so much to a garden: placid stillness, sparkling fountains, tumbling waterfalls and the diversity of beautiful plants that can only be grown under aquatic conditions.

Also, constructing a garden pool is not the laborious task that it once was. The pool still has to be excavated, of course, but the use of concrete is no longer a necessity. Modern prefabricated pools enable even the less energetic and expert to construct a water garden.

SITING THE POOL

The selection of a suitable site for the water garden is of prime importance. Apart from the fact that a pool is difficult to move after construction if you subsequently think that it would look better elsewhere, correct siting is also of vital importance for the well-being of its stock of plants and fish.

If a bad site is chosen and the plants do not prosper, the fish will not be happy and the whole watery environment will become unbalanced. This leads to problems such as discoloured or algae-laden water and no amount of interference by the gardener with proprietary pool clearers and algaecides will create a balance.

To obtain healthy and vigorous plant growth, and subsequently an attractive clear pool with sparkling water, it is essential to situate it in an open sunny position. All aquatic plants enjoy full sunlight.

A little shelter is useful to protect marginal plants from being toppled into the water by the wind. Usually potted in purpose-made aquatic planting baskets and grown in the shallow areas of the pool, marginal subjects often become top-heavy and are then easily dislodged by the wind. Shelter from the prevailing wind also helps prevent all the fallen leaves in the neighbourhood from being blown into the water.

Shade above the pool should be avoided, but that provided by waterlily pads directly beneath the surface of the water is of great value.

RIGHT A natural looking pool, sited where it can reflect mature trees in the background. A lush growth of water plants further integrates the pool into its garden setting and provides sculptural interest in pleasing contrast to the colourful shrub border beyond.

FAR RIGHT The rectangular shape of this attractive pool is effectively softened by small, rounded plant groupings in shades of pink, offset by the cool green foliage.

This helps to reduce the sunlight falling beneath the surface of the water and therefore makes life difficult for water-discolouring algae, as well as providing shade for goldfish which do not relish open clear water on hot summer afternoons.

Visual appeal Although it is important to position the pool in the correct place in order to ensure its continued success, its position from a visual viewpoint comes a close second, for a badly placed pool detracts from the general garden scene rather than enhancing it.

Gardeners often know that their pool is badly placed, but are never quite clear why. To understand the properties of water we must look at how it occurs in nature. Seldom is it found at a higher level than the surrounding ground, unless trapped among rocky crags on a mountainside. Usually it lies at rest in the lowest part of the landscape, reflecting all around it. In the garden we should follow nature as closely as possible to create a visually attractive feature.

Before excavating the hole you can obtain some idea of how the pool will look by spreading a length of rope or hose-pipe on the ground in the shape intended. This can be moved about at will until a satisfactory effect has been achieved. Pegs should then be placed at strategic points so that the outline of the chosen shape can be maintained.

Creating an illusion When it comes to siting a pool, rarely are all other aspects compatible with what is most desirable. Existing trees are, perhaps, at the lowest part of the garden and the only open situation is exposed to the prevailing winds. When such is the case, illusions have to be created and the existing situation ignored.

Discreet shelter can be provided by grouping decorative shrubs in the path of the wind so that they do not appear as a screen. When the best position in the open is not one at the lowest part of the garden, it is often possible to distribute the excavated soil so that such an illusion is created. Sometimes the placing of an occasional shrub or group of herbaceous plants is needed to separate the pool from surrounding land that is on a higher level.

Apart from the shading problem that they create, certain trees are undesirable in the vicinity of a water garden, even though they may look very attractive. Traditional weeping trees are not poolside plants, but riverside dwellers where their falling leaves are washed away by the fast-flowing water. In a pool leaves collect, decompose and produce noxious gases, those of the weeping willow containing a particularly unpleasant toxin akin to aspirin which will kill the fish.

All members of the plum and cherry family are the over-wintering host of the waterlily aphis and should be avoided, or sprayed during the winter with tar acid wash.

POOL DESIGN

The overall design that a gardener selects for a pool is a matter of personal choice. To conform to accepted standards of landscape design a formal setting should accommodate a formal pool, while an informal garden should play host to an informal pool. There are no hard and fast rules concerning design, but if basic principles are not adopted, the effect may well be as disastrous as a pool at the pinnacle of an undulating landscape, as outlined in the previous chapter.

Formality In a formal setting the surface design of the pool should conform with its surroundings. It should, therefore, be of a definite mathematical shape or shapes, consisting of a rectangle, square, oval or circle – or a combination of such shapes, but each arranged so that the overall effect is one of equilibrium. Fountains and ornaments should be similarly placed so that when viewed from any angle the effect is harmonious.

The materials from which the pool is constructed must be consistent throughout and the lines created, whether by paving or coping, pronounced and severe. It is possible to have a raised formal pool without causing visual offence and also a sunken pool, or one adjoining a wall, provided that the lines are formal in every plane.

In a formal pool planting is as important as the structural design. There is not only the necessity of including every component to create a healthy balance, but also the careful placing of every individual plant. An understanding of the habits of aquatic plants with architectural qualities is vital if the pool is to present a happy picture from the outset. A picture it is, for the plants provide the frame and the water the canvas, a reflective canvas in which the strategic placing of deep water aquatics will make or mar the overall effect you are striving for.

Open water in the formal pool is essential to allow for reflections, whether they be off nearby trees or the sky or, what is more likely, the plants which frame it.

Informality There are no rules that govern the overall surface design of a pool in an informal setting, but in practical terms it is better to have a pool without fussy corners as these are difficult to maintain. The most satisfactory informal pool will have sweeping arcs and curves that are pleasing to the eye and not too difficult to construct. The pool should also blend into the surroundings and, where possible, the edge can be disguised with creeping plants like brooklime, rupturewort and creeping jenny.

Many informal pools are sited close to a rock garden. Whenever possible bring the two together to create a unit, rather than give them separate identities. At the edge of the pool alpines and aquatics can mingle together. Planting in an informal pool is even more complicated than in a formal setting, for here the plants are artificially arranged so that the effect is that of a natural site.

Natural water Very few gardeners have the benefit of a natural pool in their garden. Those that are fortunate enough to be proud owners of natural water must take care not to

spoil such an asset. Nature has a way of doing things correctly and most natural ponds have evolved a shape without the interference of man. It is best, therefore, to leave it alone. Usually, a natural pool can be further enhanced only by sympathetic planting.

Depth While it is important to achieve an attractive overall aspect to the pool, all the planning will have been pointless if the internal structure is not satisfactory. Plants will not flourish in hostile depths, nor will fish be very happy.

Each group of aquatic plants has a minimum depth at which it will flourish and a maximum depth beyond which it will deteriorate. Most waterlilies and other deep water aquatics require a minimum depth of 45cm (1½ft) if they are to prosper, while few marginal plants will tolerate any greater depth than 23cm (9in), the majority, in fact, preferring shallower water. In order to ensure the survival of popular

TOP An attractive formal design. | **ABOVE** Carefully planned informality.

pool fish, a minimum depth at one point in the pool of 45cm (1½ft) is necessary.

When a lined or concrete pool is contemplated it is wise to look first of all at the plants that you would like to grow and then design the pool to suit their requirements. When making the calculations for various depths, bear in mind that a traditional planting basket is 15cm (6in) deep and therefore a shelf for marginal plants, for example, should be at least 23cm (9in) below the surface if their roots are to be covered with any significant amount of water.

POOL CONSTRUCTION

With the advent of modern materials the construction of a garden pool is not the hazardous and laborious task that it was once. It is true that the pool still has to be excavated, but the use of concrete – although still satisfactory – is no longer a necessity. The modern prefabricated pools allow the less energetic and expert to construct a satisfactory water garden without too much effort.

POOL LINERS

The pool liner is the most versatile of pond-building materials. Consisting of a sheet of waterproof material, it is used to line the excavation, thus forming a waterproof skin. There are so many different kinds available that there is one to suit every need and pocket.

Polythene liners These are the cheapest of all. They are usually of 500 gauge polythene, come in bright blue, or sometimes stone colour, and are readily available from supermarkets and garden centres prepacked in colourful packages for instant sales' appeal. While being inexpensive and so hopefully encouraging the most reluctant gardener to dabble in water gardening, they are the least durable, seldom having a useful life of more than three years.

The major drawback is that they perish unless kept totally immersed in water. This is difficult to achieve as in the best regulated and maintained pools a gap periodically appears between water level and ground level during hot weather when evaporation takes place. This narrow band of exposed polythene then breaks down in sunlight, becoming brittle and cracking up. Leaks start to occur and in severe cases the top of the liner becomes detached from the lower part. The most useful role for a polythene liner is as a temporary home for fish and plants when the main pool is being cleaned out.

Rubber and PVC liners These are more permanent kinds of liner, especially the heavy gauge rubber sort which is often used for lining boating lakes and irrigation lagoons. It is expensive, but the most durable kind, withstanding weather and only letting the gardener down if punctured with a sharp object; even then, easily repaired. This is not the case with the PVC type, although repair kits are freely available. Once such a liner is punctured it is better replaced. Modern PVC liners are like heavy gauge polythene, but more supple, and most are reinforced with a Terylene web. They have a long life if carefully handled and are available in a range of colours that includes blue, stone and imitation pebble.

Calculating the size It may be a surprise to find out how much larger the liner must be when compared with the size of pool you envisage. It must be remembered that it is not just the overall depth, length and breadth that have to be considered, but the width of marginal shelves and the necessary overlap.

A pool of irregular shape is even more complicated, for then the calculations have to be based upon the dimensions of a rectangle that will embrace the most distant parts of the excavation. An adequate surplus must always be allowed around the pool edge to ensure that the liner can be successfully secured.

Installation All liners are treated in a similar manner. It is just the polythene kind that presents a few problems, mainly because of its lack of elasticity. In order to have as much flexibility as possible it is essential to spread out a polythene liner to soften up in the sun.

1. Mark out the pool shape with rope or string and, when it is right, secure with pegs.

2. Carefully remove the turf in sections from inside and around the shape; set aside.

3. First excavate the pool area to required shelf depth. Check that the base is level.

4. Use the rope or string to mark the shelf outline, making this a consistent width

5. Excavate the central, deep area. Again, remember to check that the base is absolutely level.

6. Spread a layer of sand across the base to remove any irregularities and protect liner.

7. Place the liner across pool area so that it overlaps all round; weight down the edges.

8. Run water on to the liner, releasing it slowly by moving weights, until full. Trim.

9. Conceal liner's edge with turf or paving slabs, placed to slightly overlap the edge.

The hole should be excavated with sloping sides and a marginal shelf incorporated if required. Check with a spirit level and then scour the hole for sticks and stones or indeed any other object that is likely to puncture the liner once the pressure of water is holding it close against the contours of the excavation. In any event it is advisable to spread a layer of sand over the base of the excavation to act as a cushion, while on really stony soils wads of dampened newspaper pressed against the walls will give similar protection. Polythene liners have to be installed in the empty excavation prior to the addition of water instead of simultaneously, because they have little elasticity.

The other kinds, being more flexible, merely need to be spread out evenly over the hole and then water is allowed to pour into the centre. The out-spread liner is weighed down all round the edge by stones and as the pressure of the water builds up in the pool these stones are slowly removed so that the liner fits snug and tightly to the excavation. As the pool fills, any wrinkles that appear in the liner should be carefully smoothed out or camouflaged, for once it is secured into place it will be impossible to straighten out.

When the pool has filled, the top overlap should be trimmed and the liner secured to the ground before covering the edge with paving or turf. As pool liners are not harmful to aquatic life, stocking with plants can begin almost immediately.

GLASS FIBRE POOLS

The most popular method of making a permanent pool nowadays is by using a pre-formed glass fibre or vacuum-formed plastic shape. The latter, while cheap, is not ideal and is often quite difficult to install satisfactorily. Well-made glass fibre pools are difficult to surpass, for they are durable, non-toxic and reasonably easily installed.

Choosing a shape While the surface shape of a pre-formed pool need cause little concern, the correct internal structure is vital. Sadly, most manufacturers of glass fibre pools are not gardeners, nor have they studied the habits and requirements of any plants that the pools they manufacture are to accommodate. With few exceptions the marginal shelves are narrow or non-existent. Such pools are hopeless for most aquatic plants and should be avoided. Those that have a deep area and a shallow end rather than a marginal shelf are usually the best. The only slight drawback is that all the marginal subjects have to be clustered in the shallow end.

The rock pool It is very easy for the uninitiated to be tempted to purchase a rock pool. The small size and modest price are great attractions, but this kind of pool is not designed for the cultivation of aquatics or the maintenance of fish. It is manufactured to serve as a feeder pool at the summit of a rock garden, or similar raised feature, from which water disperses down a cascade or waterfall. It may be possible to establish one of the tiny rushes and a clump of submerged oxygenating plants in such a pool, but goldfish are definitely out, although an odd snail or two would not come to any harm there.

Digging the hole If you go to a garden centre and ask the salesman how to install your newly acquired glass fibre pool, it is likely that he will say that when you get it home you dig a hole to the shape. If

A glass fibre pool should have a generous shallow shelf or shelves for marginal plants. These pre-formed shapes are available in a good range of shapes and sizes and they are very durable.

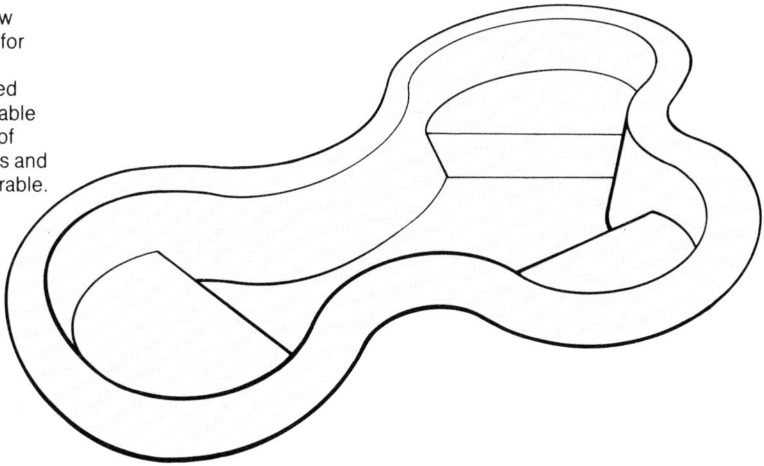

you have ever attempted this you will know that is a flight of fancy and impossible to achieve. What must be done is to dig a hole of sufficient length, breadth and depth to accommodate the extreme dimensions of the pool, the shallow end being supported by bricks. Ensure that the hole not only accommodates the pool, but allows sufficient space around the edge for proper back-filling.

Installing the pool Having excavated a suitable hole, place the pool in it and carefully level it from side to side and end to end with the aid of a straight plank and a spirit level, while ensuring adequate support under the shallow end. At this stage, the rim of the pool should not be level with the surrounding ground, for with the steady pressure of back-filling it will inevitably rise. Allow a couple of centimetres for this process, thus starting with the pool that much below the level of the surrounding soil.

If the excavated soil is fairly even and friable it can be used for back-filling. In most cases however, this will not be the case so, rather than struggle and make an unsatisfactory job, use river sand, fine grit or some other uniform material that will flow easily. Not only is the task simplified, but air pockets are less likely to arise and so pressure from within the pool, such as a heavy foot when the pool is cleaned out, will not cause the glass fibre surface to fracture and consequently leak.

The edge of the pool can be finished off with paving slabs, or else turf can be brought up to the surround. In this case it is important that the fibrous part of the turf is kept in close contact with the water so that the turf does not dry out.

Vacuum-formed plastic pools are very similar to the glass fibre kind, but being less rigid are much more difficult to install properly. Excavation of the hole follows the same principle, but the back-filling is more complicated. Also, as these pools are so flexible, it is important to keep them rigid by adding water as the back-filling takes place. This holds the pool down and therefore no allowance need be made for the fractional rising of the pool.

CONCRETE POOLS

Making a concrete pool cannot be described as anything other than hard work. However, in the last analysis if you have the skill and time available to build one it is probably still the most permanent form of construction. Apart from being durable, after a couple of seasons it can take on a completely natural look. Limitations are only placed upon the size and shape of the pool by the materials used. It is therefore desirable that a pool should have the minimum of fussy niches and contortions (these would require complicated shuttering), gently sloping sides, and a surface area no greater than available labour can concrete in a single day.

Excavating the hole When digging a hole for a concrete pool, bear in mind that the overall excavation will need to be 15cm (6in) larger than the finished size of the pool, to allow for the thickness of concrete. It should be shaped so that there are no acute angles and the sides have no more of a slope than can be managed without the necessity of shuttering. When complete, the sides of the hole and the floor must be firmly rammed to avoid subsidence later. The excavation can then be lined with heavy gauge builder's polythene before concreting takes place. The polythene is an additional minimal insurance against leakage and prevents moisture from the concrete soaking into the soil and drying out the concrete too rapidly. The quick drying of concrete can lead to hair cracks appearing in the surface.

Preparing the concrete Ideally you should try to purchase ready mixed concrete from a wagon. This will be evenly mixed, of uniform consistency and, on request, will have had waterproofing powder added. The disadvantage is that it will arrive on the designated day, wet or fine, and may have to be discharged a considerable distance from the site.

Mixing by hand is tedious, but a good job can be done with care. A suitable mixture consists of one part by volume of cement, two parts sand and four parts of gravel (¾in chippings). This is mixed with a shovel in its dry state until it is of a uniform grey colour. If a waterproofing powder is to be added this should be done before the material is mixed with water. Water is subsequently added and the mixture turned backwards and forwards until of a stiff consistency and even, dark grey colour. To test if it is ready for use, introduce a shovel and move it up and down in a series of jerks. If the ridges that are produced remain, then the concrete is ready to be laid.

Laying the concrete The initial layer of concrete is spread evenly over the floor of the pool and up the sides to a depth of 10cm (4in). Large mesh wire netting, such as that used on poultry farms, is then pressed into the wet concrete to act as a reinforcement. Another 5cm (2in) of concrete is then spread over this and smoothed out with a plasterer's trowel to give a pleasing finish.

Once any lingering surface water has dispersed, the concrete should be allowed to dry slowly to prevent hair cracks from appearing. Small areas can be covered with damp hessian sacks, but where this is impossible, a watering can with a fine rose attachment can be used at regular intervals to sprinkle the surface of the concrete. This only needs to be done for a couple of days until the concrete has started to set firmly.

Making it safe One of the undisputed disadvantages of using concrete for pool construction is the fact that when water is run into the pool free lime is released. This is harmful in varying degrees to both plants and fish and therefore should be neutralised. A sealant, such as the universally available 'Silglaze', will do the job. This is a white powder that is mixed with water and then painted on the dry surface of the concrete. Apart from neutralising the lime it also seals the concrete.

Rubber-based and liquid plastic paints can also play a role in preventing the escape of free lime, although their main purpose is as a waterproof pond sealant. Available in a variety of colours, these must only be applied after a suitable primer. Without the primer, the paint will just peel away. Once the pool has been sealed and protected against the effects of free lime it can be planted immediately.

1. When digging the hole for a concrete pool, allow extra depth and width to accommodate the thickness of the concrete. Avoid acute angles or slopes.
2. When you have dug out to required dimensions, ram the floor hard to avoid later subsidence.
3. Line the excavated area with heavy gauge builders' polythene to safeguard against wet concrete leaking into the soil or drying out too soon
4. If shuttering *is* required, it should be erected at this stage and infilled.
5. Otherwise, reinforce concrete with large-mesh wire netting, pressed into the still wet mixture.
6. Spread another 5cm (2in) of concrete over the first layer and use a trowel to achieve a smooth finish. Ensure that concrete does not dry out too quickly, as described in the main text, left.

FOUNTAINS AND WATERFALLS

Moving water in the garden adds a magical touch. Not just the visual appeal of a fountain spray in the sunlight or the frothing and tumbling of water down a cascade, but the marvellous tinkling and splashing that accompanies it. A garden should alert all the senses. Water does this in the most pleasant of ways.

It is important to remember, however, that when the fountain plays waterlilies sulk and the water gardener must decide his priorities. Waterlilies and similar deep water aquatics are naturally inhabitants of pools and quiet backwaters where they remain undisturbed. Constant turbulence in the water will mean that within a season they have faded away. Only in a large pool where the plants can be distanced from such mayhem will both exist in harmony.

Choosing a pump Selecting a suitable pump is like buying a new car. You really have got to know what you are doing and so it is prudent to study the catalogues of two or three water gardening specialists and see what they are offering. Most specialists offer similar pumps of a submersible nature and these will be the kind from which to choose.

Reliability is vital, but almost equally important is the choice of a pump that will produce a satisfactory flow for the project in hand. In order to put a 15cm (6in) continuous flow of water across an average cascade unit, a capacity of 1365 litres (300 gals) an hour is needed.

If you are not able to visualise how much water is going to be required for your particular waterfall, run a garden hose over the feature for one minute and collect the water in a container. Measure the amount collected in pints, multiply by 7.5 and you will arrive at the gallonage per hour. A pump of suitable capacity can then be chosen.

There are two kinds of pumps that are manufactured for garden pools, the submersible and the surface. The latter is really for pumping large quantities of water and needs to be accommodated in a special small building, so it has its limitations for the home gardener. The majority of gardeners obtain the totally submersible pump, as this is easily installed and quite capable of producing a decent fountain or waterfall and, in some cases, both these features together.

The fountain This can be created quite simply by using a submersible pump and standing it on a firm base within the pool, with the outlet jet just beneath the water. Special heads are available for attachment to the outlet, each with holes that give different spray patterns.

LEFT A traditional fountain with forceful jets created by a submersible pump. BELOW A pebble fountain is a safe, attractive feature for the small garden, and where the stones are splashed by water, there will be a bonus of subtly changing colours on their surfaces. RIGHT This tiny, circular pool edged by shaped stone flags, uses the fountain as a centrepiece.

RIGHT Carefully chosen foliage gives a pleasing aspect to this tiny pool. The creamy waterlily provides an ideal contrast to the sculptural shapes of the hosta leaves and surrounding rocks.

BELOW Moving water adds magic and music to a garden, whether it be the soft whisper of a stream over pebbles or, as here, the more forceful play of a waterfall.

As submersible pumps are electrical, it is sensible to seek the advice of an electrician, as the mixture of electricity and water is potentially lethal. The pump usually comes with a considerable length of waterproof cable. This should be fastened to the output cable by means of a special waterproof connector. If it is possible, this connector should be situated beneath one of the paving slabs around the pool as this gives easy access when the pump is removed during the winter and also provides some protection for the joint.

The waterfall A simple cascade or waterfall can be taken from a submersible pump, either separately or simultaneously with a fountain. A length of hosepipe is connected to the pump outlet and then hidden close by the waterfall unit so that

ABOVE Here, a submersible pump is used to create a waterfall flowing down through two small, stepped pools into a third that contains a fountain powered by the same pump.
BELOW A gentle waterfall cascading down over rocky "steps" into a small garden pool. This is achieved by using the same principle.

the end just pours water in at the top. As with the fountain, a submersible pump draws water in one end and then pushes it out the other, merely circulating it.

The waterfall unit itself can be made with concrete or a pool liner, but the simplest and most satisfactory waterfall is constructed using a pre-formed glass fibre length. Although initially it may look quite stark, it is possible to disguise the more objectionable parts with stones and plants. This minor inconvenience is compensated for by the guaranteed waterproofing of the run and the correct pushing and manipulating of water to give a natural effect. One very important factor to bear in mind when building a waterfall with a prefabricated unit, is that it should go in accurately and be absolutely level from side to side.

Using a filter While achieving a natural balance is the aim of the keen water gardener, this is not done overnight. Many gardeners consider clear water to be a matter of pride and so in the initial stages of establishment – and regretfully later on too – install a pool filter. This is attached to the suction end of the pump and generally consists of a flat pad in a tray through which water is drawn in the normal pumping action. The changeable mat is regularly inspected and cleaned, and only crystal clear water is discharged by the pump.

PLANTING THE POOL

Once the time to plant the pool has arrived the really hard work has been completed. Choosing suitable plants is a joy, but beware of turning the pool into a plant collection. To obtain the best effect plant two or three plants of one kind in an individual planting basket, and do restrict the number of baskets, for open space is just as important.

Creating a balance This is of paramount importance and visual requirements must follow those necessary to produce a happy and healthy environment. There is a rough and ready formula that applies to garden pools and the successful establishment of an harmonious balance. It is not based upon scientific study, but on the observations over many years of gardeners who have developed this useful rule of thumb. It is based upon the total surface area of the pool, excluding the marginal shelves, and suggests that submerged oxygenating plants – which are usually sold as bunches of unrooted cuttings – should be planted at the rate of one bunch to 0.09sq.m (1sq.ft). That is not to say that they must be distributed at appropriate intervals across the pool floor, the bunch can be planted in a single basket, but the quantity of plant material used for a given surface area is critical.

LEFT The charming stone figure provides a focal point.
ABOVE The use of aquatic planting baskets is essential to house the plants.
BELOW Pond with *Aponogeton distachyus*, deserving of a place in any water garden.

Similarly with fish, the rate per 0.09sq.m (1sq.ft) is 5cm (2in) of fish nose to tail, although in a pool where no further fish raising is anticipated it is possible to increase that length to 15cm (6in).

The surface of the pool should also be shaded. For a successful balance to be established, approximately one third of the surface should be covered with the foliage of floating and deep water aquatics.

How plants help The most important plants for creating a balance in a pool are the submerged oxygenating plants (see page 42 for descriptions of recommended kinds). Uninspiring in appearance, it is these 'weeds', as we affectionately call them, that hold the key to natural balance. Apart from providing oxygen for fish and other livestock, they compete for mineral salts in the water, and being higher plants than the tiny free-floating algae, deprive them of nourishment by utilising all the dissolved salts.

Light is also vital for the proper development of green plants, so if light can be excluded from beneath the surface of the water, the green water-discolouring algae will have a tough time. It is important not to skimp on the introduction of these plants, even though many are rather dull, for without them the pool would be a most unsavoury place.

Do not be deluded into thinking that as the submerged oxygenating plants provide oxygen it is this which keeps the water clear. The fact that the plants are called oxygenating is incidental and a little misleading, giving some gardeners the idea that they do not need such plants if their pools are well oxygenated by fountain or waterfall. Oxygen is not the key. Competition for plant foods is the answer.

The value of fish Fish in a pool are like the icing on the cake. They enliven a very pleasant picture, providing movement and colour in a way which cannot be achieved elsewhere in the garden. Apart from their visual appeal, they confer practical benefits upon the gardener, devouring all manner of aquatic insect pests, including the ubiquitous mosquito.

Enhancing the pool As with most other parts of the garden, the plants are what give a feature character. Once the essential pool plants are established you can consider adding those that are grown purely for decoration.

Try to find something that will flower for most of the spring and summer. No individual aquatic plant could perform such a feat, but there are several very attractive long-flowering kinds that could be planted to bloom in sequence.

Foliage should not be forgotten either. Look at colour, form and habit. In the pool more than anywhere else in the garden shapes are important, for it is not just their immediate visual impact that enhances the picture but that of their reflections as well.

Try to tie the pool to the rest of the garden by allowing pool plants to colonise damp soil at the water's edge and conversely let garden plants march to the edge of the pool if they have the desire. The newly constructed garden pool is a watery canvas which just requires the artistic gardener to pick up his plants and place them sympathetically. Once the framework and background are established, you can enliven the foreground with some colourful fish.

Choosing your plants Recommended kinds of the various types of plant used in pool and waterside gardening and described here are given on pages 38-47.

Waterlilies and deep water aquatics Apart from the waterlilies (*Nymphaea*) there are a number of other deep water aquatics that merit consideration. All provide a certain amount of floating foliage and are essential for creating a suitable area of water surface shade to ensure a good balance in the pool. In addition, waterlilies flower almost continuously from early summer until the first autumn frosts.

The planting season for waterlilies and other deep water aquatics extends from spring until late summer, the plants being established in baskets of good clean garden soil with just their terminal shoots protruding above the surface.

When collecting soil prior to planting it is important to avoid mixing old leaves or weeds with it as these are likely to decompose and pollute the water. Soil from the vegetable garden or any other area that has been recently dressed with artificial fertiliser should also be avoided as this will cause algae to appear in the pool and lead to all kinds of associated problems.

Once a plant has been planted in a basket the soil should be covered with about 1cm (½in) of fine pea gravel. This will prevent fish from stirring up the compost in their quest for aquatic insect life. In any event it is useful to soak the basket thoroughly with water from a can with a fine rose attachment. This drives out all the air and prevents soil and other debris from escaping into the water.

FAR LEFT *Nymphaea* 'Sunrise', one of the finest yellow waterlilies for the deeper pool.
LEFT Clear water in the pool depends upon the correct balance of submerged plants and floating foliage.
ABOVE Waterlilies are the queens of the garden pool, flowering all summer long.

Most gardeners remove the adult leaves from waterlilies and similar lily-like aquatics before planting. This deprives them of a buoyancy aid and enables them to become established so much quicker. Retaining old floating leaves will often have the effect of lifting plants right out of their containers.

When placing waterlilies in the pool it is essential to site them as far

ABOVE The subtle blending of foliage colour and contrast provides a lovely background for this colourful pool with grassy banks.

RIGHT *Iris laevigata* 'Variegata', a choice marginal plant.
BELOW RIGHT *Hemerocallis* 'Pink Prelude', a popular daylily.

away from moving water as possible. The other deep water aquatics are more tolerant and can therefore be placed accordingly.

In larger natural or established water gardens, where there is earth on the floor of the pool, deep water aquatics and waterlilies can be planted more easily by fastening up individual plants in hessian squares, packing round the rootstock with good clean, heavy soil, and then lowering the package into place. Eventually the roots will penetrate the hessian and ramify the surrounding silt and soil.

Floating plants These make a major contribution to the balance of the pool by providing surface shade. Along with the deep water aquatics they provide a cool haven for ornamental fish on a hot summer's day. They also effectively reduce the intensity of light beneath the water, thereby making it difficult for primitive green water-discolouring algae to become established. Floating plants and submerged oxygenating plants are the mainstays of a good natural balance within the pool.

Floating plants require little special attention, although most gardeners remove a small portion, or a few winter buds, to the safety of a frost-free place so that they can be hastened into growth during the spring. The planting of floating aquatics consists of tossing the plants on to the surface of the water.

Their partners in the quest for a balanced pool – the submerged oxygenating plants – are often treated in the same manner. This is rarely successful as the plants are almost exclusively supplied as bunches of rootless cuttings fastened together with a strip of lead. Although they may seem to be clinging precariously to life, once introduced to the water they grow away quickly. However, it is important for them to have something to root into in order to become anchored.

In a well established pool there is often enough accumulated debris on the pool floor to allow anchorage, but in a freshly established water garden it is preferable to plant the bunches in proper aquatic planting baskets in good clean garden soil. It is vital that the lead strip attached to the base of the cuttings is completely buried in the soil or else the tops of the cuttings will become detached as the lead rots through their stems. A topdressing of clean pea gravel is also essential to prevent the soil from being stirred up.

1. When planting the basket, thread a length of strong string through the mesh at each of the corners, as above.

2. If you want to site the basket at the deepest point of the pool, you may need to support the basket on bricks.

3. As the filled basket will weigh quite heavy, you will need assistance in order to lower it into the pool evenly.

Marginal plants These are aquatics which grow in mud or shallow water towards the edge of the pool. Planting is the same as advocated for waterlilies, except that instead of always being planted in baskets, they are not infrequently established directly into soil that has been spread along the marginal shelf. Marginal plants should ideally be planted in groups of three or four of the same kind as this gives a more pleasing and natural effect.

Bog garden plants A bog garden is usually constructed alongside a pool and provides a home for those plants that enjoy moist conditions, but will not tolerate standing water. Some are popularly grown in moist parts of the herbaceous border. All those included on pages 45-7 are perennial and need dividing regularly every three or four years if they are to maintain vigour and quality of flower. All can be planted during the dormant season, although some are available container grown from nurseries and garden centres all the year through.

PLANT PROPAGATION

Most gardeners like to raise a few plants, if only to give away to friends. Just because aquatic plants live in water it does not mean to say that they are any more difficult to increase than their land-dwelling cousins. Special conditions are not required, most young water plants can be raised in a large household bowl in a cold frame or greenhouse.

Waterlilies from eyes It is relatively simple to raise waterlilies from 'eyes', even though it takes two or more years to produce a flowering size crown. The eyes are really latent growing points which occur with varying frequency along the scrambling roots of mature waterlilies. If these are removed at the time when the adult plant is being divided or re-planted, they can be rooted and grown into flowering-size plants, thus increasing your stocks.

The ideal period is during late spring or early summer, but propagation can continue until late summer. Most eyes have to be removed with a knife, although some can be detached by hand. Raw surfaces should be dressed with sulphur or charcoal to prevent fungal infection, and the severed eyes potted individually in good clean garden soil and stood in a bowl of water. The adult plant can be returned to its place in the pool.

As the emerging leaf stalks lengthen, the water level should be raised. The plants must then be potted on progressively until large enough to be accommodated in a proper planting basket.

Plants from seed A few of the miniature waterlilies, like the ever popular *Nymphaea pygmaea* 'Alba', have to be increased from seed. To be successful, seed must be fresh and have been kept moist. Dried seed is most unlikely to germinate. Freshly harvested seed is mixed in with a thick jelly-like substance from which it is virtually impossible to remove the individual seeds. In order to avoid damage, it is advisable to sow the seeds with the jelly. A good clean garden soil, as recommended for eyes, should be used, and the water level in the bowl should just cover the surface of the compost.

The first seedlings appear after a couple of weeks and look like small translucent liverworts. At this time they are vulnerable to damage by filamentous algae, which should be controlled by the regular use of an algaecide. Once the seedlings are producing floating foliage they are large enough to be pricked out into trays in the usual manner, and eventually can be transferred to individual pots.

Most other aquatic plants can be dealt with in a similar way, although a number such as *Pontederia cordata* and *Aponogeton distachyus* should not be allowed to dry out and must be sown fresh. Others such as *Myosotis scorpioides* and *Alisma plantago-aquatica* can be stored for a while and will still germinate satisfactorily.

Plants from cuttings Creeping aquatics, like *Veronica beccabunga* and *Menyanthes trifoliata*, are easily grown from short stem cuttings taken at any time during the growing season. These should be about 5cm (2in) long and inserted in a tray of mud. Once rooting takes place, the plants are potted individually.

Plants by division Most of the reeds and rushes, together with aquatic irises and marsh marigolds, can be increased by division. They need thinning out periodically in any event, mature plants being carefully lifted and divided in the same way as ordinary herbaceous perennials. Two small hand forks placed back to back in the centre of a clump, then prised apart will separate tough plants. Select healthy young outer shoots for propagation.

RIGHT View of replanted young lily, showing correct ratio of planting mediums.

1. Overgrown plants such as this waterlily can be divided with the aid of a sharp knife to make more plants.

2. After washing and trimming the roots slightly, replant the parent plant and its offspring in separate baskets.

3. As when dealing with any perennial, centre the plant in the basket and take care to firm it well in.

4. After planting, add a 2.5cm (1in) layer of pebbles to keep the soil in place once the basket has been submerged.

1. When a new plantlet produced by a tropical waterlily leaf produces roots, cut round the plantlet as shown.

2. Pin down plantlet over a 10cm (4in) pot of soil. Submerge below 5cm (2in) water. Transplant when rooted.

STOCKING WITH ANIMAL LIFE

It is very important that any fish that are introduced to the pool are healthy. Fish living in a garden pool are occupying what is generally a clean and disease-free environment. The introduction of a single diseased fish can rapidly decimate the rest of the fish population. For this reason, it is always prudent to quarantine newly acquired fish for a couple of weeks in a tub or aquarium before putting them in the pool.

Choosing fish Ornamental pool fish that are swimming around happily in the dealer's tank and have upright fins and a bright eye, can usually be relied upon to be in good health. Treat any slow swimming or excessively speedy fish with caution and whenever possible avoid those that have lost a few scales as such wounds are open to infection by fungal diseases.

It is also prudent to transport fish only during cool weather. Never subject fish to a journey home in a polythene bag in a hot car on a bright summer day. This particularly applies to golden and silver orfe which have a high oxygen requirement and succumb very quickly.

No more than a total length of 15cm (6in) of fish (including the tail) should be permitted for every 0.09sq.m (1sq.ft) of pool surface area. A rate of one third of that would be much more satisfactory (5cm to 0.09 sq.m/2in to 1 sq. ft) and would ensure steady growth amongst the fish and increase the likelihood of successful breeding taking place.

The size of the individual fish is not important, it is the total combined body length of the fish against the total amount of water surface area available upon which the formula is based. Many small fish are infinitely superior to a few large individuals. Diversity of colour and type will add considerable interest to the watery picture.

Before contemplating the stocking of a newly planted pool with fish, allow at least three weeks to pass so that the plants can become established. Early introductions try to stir up the compost and pull the plants about. Plaintive wailings from impatient children should be resisted at all costs if the pool is to remain clear and balanced from the outset.

All the popular ornamental pool fish co-exist quite happily together. It is only newly hatched fry that are eaten by the adults.

Goldfish Most people are familiar with this common ornamental fish which is available in red, orange, white and all shades between. It is a hardy character and capable of attaining quite a substantial size when given plenty of room. Indeed, the small goldfish of the goldfish bowl, if allowed the freedom of a garden pool, will grow quickly into

an adult fish. Apart from conventional goldfish, there are long-tailed varieties called Comet-Longtails and transparent scaled kinds in bright mixed colours called Shubunkins.

Carp The majority of fish encountered in the garden pool are members of the carp family. Common goldfish and shubunkins are really derived from a species of carp. Those referred to by gardeners as carp include many undesirable coarse fish that are uninteresting in appearance and boisterous in the small pool. The only two kinds to consider are the Chinese Red Carp or Higoi and the Japanese Nishiki-Koi or Koi carp. The Higoi is a meaty salmon-pink coloured fish with a blunt head and pendant barbels, while the Koi is of similar shape and appearance but with brightly coloured scales that often have a metallic lustre.

Orfe There are both golden and silver orfe, but it is only the former which is widely available. This is a sleek surface swimming fish of an orange-pink colour which, when mature, looks like a well proportioned carrot swimming in the water. Orfe are shoal fish which should be introduced in threes or fours at least.

Raising fish When fish start breeding in the garden pool it is generally a sign that all is well. However, for the gardener it is a time of concern, for here swimming in the water are myriad young fish which are being preyed upon each day. The instinct to save every individual is strong, but should be resisted, for in the natural way of things the weaker and smaller progeny will provide nourishment for other inhabitants. Usually sufficient young fry escape to grow into young fish and then take their place alongside their parents in the general rough and tumble of the pool. Indeed, the pool owner with a good natural balance in his water garden will usually raise a few youngsters each year without giving the fish any help.

LEFT A pool of colourful goldfish. **ABOVE** Koi carp, King of the pool.

RIGHT Golden orfe, sleek surface swimmers, are happiest in shoals.

Most water gardeners, though, like to breed fish as an integral part of pool management. Those intent upon doing this usually select pairs of breeding fish at the outset and ensure that there is sufficient underwater foliage for the deposition of spawn.

The breeding season lasts from late spring to late summer and it depends largely upon the intensity of light and warmth of the water as to when the fish will spawn. Most goldfish are capable of breeding during their second year, although any fish 8cm (3in) or more in length should be sexually active.

While most fish in the garden pool will be of the carp family, not all breed readily in this country. Like breed with like, although some of the true carp and goldfish will on occasions inter-breed. Male fish can be distinguished from female fish by their more slender body shape and the presence during the breeding season of nuptial tubercles on their gills and heads. These are like tiny white spots which disappear entirely for the winter.

Spawning This is the mating of fish in the open water, the female being chased around the pool by a male who will knock and brush against her in an effort to get her to release her spawn. When this has happened the male will deposit his milt or sperm-bearing fluid over the eggs and with any luck a union will take place.

When this has been observed, the spawn and the plants on which they were laid should be transferred to a bucket of pool water. This will be of the same chemical composition and temperature and few problems should be encountered with the emerging fry (young fishes fresh from the spawn). If you wish, the spawn can take its chance with the hungry adults. A few young fish will inevitably survive. Removing fry from the pool ensures a high percentage yield of young fish.

Looking after fry If the spawn removed from the pool is placed in a cool place with an even temperature, after three or four days it will be seen to be developing. To begin with the fry are difficult to see, looking like tiny translucent pins in the water, clinging to submerged plant foliage. Two or three weeks later they are recognisable as fish, sometimes transparent, sometimes bronze, but all eventually attaining their adult hue.

Goldfish will sometimes remain bronze for several years and then suddenly change colour. This delay in complete colour change is associated with water temperature at spawning time. The lower the water temperature at spawning, the longer it will take the progeny to attain their rightful adult hue.

Fry that usually live freely in the open pool soon find their own food, but in the sterile conditions of a sizeable bucket this is not very likely. Special baby fish foods that resemble tubes of toothpaste are available, but an equally successful food can be made from scrambled eggs. Feeding in a container should continue until the fry are 2.5cm (1in) long, when they can be returned to the pool fairly safely.

Scavenging fish and snails There is a common misconception among water gardeners that a pool will not function successfully without scavenging fish and snails. This has arisen because many pool owners believe that scavengers are living vacuum cleaners and will suck up and devour mud, debris and all the undesirable accumulation on the pool floor. What they actually do is to devour uneaten goldfish food, which if left to accumulate on the bottom of the pool would grow fungus and pollute the water. Snails feed to a limited extent upon such detritus, but are included in a pool to eat algae, particularly the filamentous kind that clings to submerged oxygenating plants and aquatic planting baskets.

Catfish and tench Scavenging fish spend their life on the floor of the pool clearing up undesirable debris. Both contenders for this place in the pool are capable of performing the task, but the catfish is, in addition, pugnacious and carnivorous. This means that as he gets larger he is likely to prey upon other fish, especially the slower swimming fancy kinds and the fry of almost every sort. Also, as he is going to spend most of his life in the hidden depths of the pool, once introduced, he is almost impossible to catch and remove without draining the pool almost completely.

The tench, on the other hand, is a much more subdued and dignified fish. He is equally unseen once in the pool, but he will not harm his fellow inmates. Tench are sleek greyish-green fish with smooth slimy bodies. There is a golden form which costs about three times as much as the common kind, but as you are unlikely to see it, its introduction is folly. The best place for the golden tench is the coldwater aquarium where it can be viewed without difficulty.

Freshwater snails There are many different aquatic snails that can be introduced to the garden pool, but only the ramshorn can be relied upon to confine its activities to grazing on algae. The common freshwater whelk or greater pond snail which is frequently offered for sale by garden centres will eat algae, but you will soon discover it is equally partial to waterlily foliage.

Tench (left) and Catfish (above) are both useful scavengers in that they will keep the pool clear of undesirable debris, but the Tench is less likely to be troublesome.

The ramshorn snail is a distinctive character with a rounded flat shell like a catherine wheel which it carries in an upright fashion on its back. The body may be black, red or white, all kinds being equally useful. The freshwater whelk, on the other hand, has a tall spiralled shell and a greyish body.

Both these snails are often introduced to the pool unwittingly as eggs on the foliage of aquatic plants. The eggs of the desirable ramshorn kind are produced in a flat pad of jelly which is often seen stuck beneath the floating foliage of deep water aquatics and waterlilies. The eggs of the freshwater whelk are produced in a small cigar-shaped cylinder of jelly which may be attached to any part of a plant. The removal of the latter type of snail at planting time will prevent a lot of problems later.

Freshwater mussels There are two kinds of freshwater mussel generally available from water garden specialists. Both are equally useful in an established pool where there is an accumulation of debris on the pool floor. The swan mussel has a brownish-green shell with a white fleshy body, while the painter's mussel has a yellowish shell with distinctive brown markings. Both draw in algae-laden water, retain the algae and discharge clear water.

Frogs, toads and newts Any, or sometimes all these characters, may take up residence in the pool. All are insectivorous and benefit the gardener considerably, feeding from time to time not only upon troublesome aquatic insect pests, but also on many other familiar garden pests as well.

All breed in the water leaving a deposition of spawn. The newts cunningly disguise their spawn, but that of frogs and toads is quite evident. All are fun to watch develop into tadpoles and ultimately adults, and the garden pool now provides the last refuge from agricultural development for several species. None do any harm in the pool and the spawn and tadpoles are regarded as a delicacy by many fish.

ABOVE Common frog, the gardener's friend.
RIGHT Frog spawn provides a delicacy for hungry fish, but sufficient escape to become adult frogs.

POND PROBLEMS

Apart from the pests and diseases that attack both plants and fish and which are described on page 35, there are a number of other problems that can arise and these need prompt attention if they are to be brought under control before real damage can occur.

Green water When the pool becomes green and pea-soup like, it is usually the result of an excessive amount of sunlight falling into the water, combined with an abundance of dissolved mineral salts. These two conditions encourage the proliferation of myriad free-floating algae which then drift about in the water like dense clouds of aquatic dust. Only by planting suitable plants in the correct ratio can this condition be alleviated permanently.

Even then it may temporarily occur during the spring when the sun shines brightly and the higher plants are not actively growing and competing for mineral salts in the water. The competition provided by sufficient submerged oxygenating plants and the shade afforded by the floating foliage of deep water aquatics and floating subjects bring about the only permanent cure, although algaecides based upon permanganate of potash will clear the water for a short period. This treatment should not, however, be undertaken during warm weather or the water will turn yellow.

Filamentous algae are a different proposition. These are known variously as silkweed, blanket weed and flannel weed and float around the pool freely in thick pads, or else

Duckweed, bane of the pool owner. Do not permit it to spread!

entangle themselves around and amongst submerged and deep water aquatics.

Removal by hand is the only way to get rid of filamentous algae, although planting submerged oxygenating plants and floating subjects in sufficient quantity will help to prevent a severe infestation. Algaecides based upon copper sulphate will kill the algae, but it is necessary to remove the dead remains or else they will decompose and pollute the water.

Dirty water This means water that is not green, but either brown or blue and often putrid. Brown water is the result of fish stirring up soil in the planting baskets. This often occurs when fish are introduced into a pool before the plants have had an opportunity to become established. The fish disturb them, often pulling them right out of the containers, which in turn brings soil up and into the water. Even the careful placing of a layer of gravel over the surface of each basket will not have the desired effect. Light soil often drifts through the lattice-work sides of the containers and creates a dirty cloud. To prevent this, always plant in baskets that are lined with hessian. This will retain the soil and yet allow the roots to escape.

Blue-black water, often with an oily film or white unpleasant scum on the surface, is usually associated with the decomposing remains of something organic. In most cases this will be a fish or mussels. Single creatures rarely cause a major problem, so when this situation arises there is something seriously wrong and the pool must be cleaned out at the earliest opportunity to discover the cause. The walls of the pool must be scrubbed, and it is an advantage if the floor can be allowed to dry out and the pool remain empty for several days. All healthy plants can be returned to the pool, but all should be thoroughly washed before reintroduction.

Cats and herons Pool owners who live in high density residential areas are not necessarily free from the attention of the heron. It seems that nothing escapes the watchful eye of this magnificent bird. When the disappearance of fish from the pool is unexplained, it is probably the result of the fishing antics of a heron.

Arriving at dawn, herons are rarely seen, catching their prey by stealth and disappearing before the gardener is awake. Fishing from the edge of the pool, they stand stock still until a fish comes into sight and then like quick-silver they make a dart for it. Fish of all sizes are equally vulnerable, although really large goldfish are often awkward to take away.

Garden centres sell heron netting for spreading over the pool, but while this is effective, it is also difficult to manage successfully. The plants grow through the netting and make general pool maintenance difficult. The simplest and cheapest method of control is to erect a series of short canes, 15cm (6in) high, from which black garden cotton or fishing line is fastened to give the effect of a low fence. Herons walk into the water when fishing and on feeling the line against their legs, will walk no further. Several sorties coming into contact with an unseen barrier will serve as a deterrent and they will go elsewhere.

Cats are not so easily prevented; all that can be done is to ensure that the paving at the edge of the pool has sufficient overhang to enable a fish to lie beneath it unobserved.

PESTS AND DISEASES

There are several pests and diseases which attack aquatic plants. None causes a really serious problem, except perhaps for waterlily root rot, but many disfigure plants and affect their productivity. General garden and pool hygiene assists in controlling some of the most pernicious ones. This is extremely important for a pool that is stocked with decorative fish cannot be sprayed with a fungicide or insecticide.

Waterlily aphid The true waterlily aphid is very troublesome, but water sprayed from a hose-pipe will knock many of the insects into the water where the fish can get at them. A winter spray with 'Clean-Up' tar acid wash of nearby plum and decorative cherry trees will kill the over-wintering population.

Caddis flies Their larvae feed on the leaves, stems, roots and flowers of aquatic plants. They also gather plant material which they mix with sand, sticks and other debris to create tiny protective shelters, so it is impossible to spray successfully against caddis fly even if there are no fish in the pool. However, in a well stocked pool the fish keep the population down.

Waterlily leaf spot There are two well known leaf spots of waterlilies, neither of which is fatal. However, they are disfiguring and can be controlled by the regular removal and burning of diseased foliage.

Waterlily root rot A damaging disease which can kill all the waterlilies in the pool. There is no cure, the affected waterlilies should be destroyed and the compost in which they were growing disposed of.

PESTS AND DISEASES OF FISH

Provided that care is taken with the introduction of fresh stock, few pests or diseases should manifest themselves upon fish in the well maintained pool. However, problems do arise, as described below.

Fungus Fungal diseases commonly attack coldwater fish around their fins and gills.

Until recently the only reliable cure that has been available to the amateur fish keeper has been sea salt. This works, but takes a long time to have any real effect. However, nowadays it is possible to obtain fungus cures based upon either malachite green or methylene blue. The victim is dipped into such a solution for a short period and then returned to the pool.

Fin and tail rot are similar propositions, except that in cases where the disease has not advanced into the flesh of the fish, tattered and badly infested parts can be trimmed away with scissors. Treatment for fungal infection is essential.

White spot disease A very common parasitic disease which causes myriad white spots to appear all over the body of the fish. This should not be confused with the display of white nuptial tubercles by mature males. These only occur on the gill plates, top of the head and close by the pectoral fins.

Fish that are only just showing signs of infestation can be treated satisfactorily with a white spot cure based upon quinine salts.

GARDENING YEAR

Once established there is a minimal amount of maintenance necessary to keep a garden pool in good order. Even though little work is required, it is very important that it is done regularly and on time. A garden pool is a vulnerable environment that needs to be observed regularly.

Spring and summer Most aquatic plants are heavy feeders and require regular feeding. This cannot be done in a haphazard fashion, for it must be remembered that once plant foods have escaped into the pool they will provide sustenance for myriad water-discolouring algae.

Special aquatic plant fertilisers are available. These are small perforated plastic sachets filled with fertiliser, which can be pushed into each basket adjacent to each plant. The fertiliser is then released where it is required and not into the water.

It is also possible to make bonemeal 'pills' which consist of small balls of clay in which bonemeal has been mixed. These too can be pushed into each basket in a similar manner.

After a period of time most aquatic plants need lifting and dividing. This usually occurs in the third or fourth year after planting. Early spring is the ideal time to undertake this task, just as the plants are starting to grow. Leave it until mid-summer and the divided plants will look unhappy and spoil the overall effect of the pool for that season.

Dividing plants is a natural way of increasing them for use in another part of the pool or for distributing to friends. While lifting and dividing it is also possible to remove the 'eyes' from waterlilies for propagation purposes and to remove short stem cuttings as well (see also page 26).

Feeding fish is a summer occupation. While it is very pleasurable, it is not usually necessary in a properly established and balanced pool to feed, although fish freshly installed in a new pool will probably be glad of a little easily acquired nourishment. Most pool owners enjoy feeding fish, and although there is no sound reason for providing artificial food, the fish will not complain about easy pickings and the pool owner will derive enormous pleasure from their antics. Take care not to distribute more food than can be comfortably devoured in twenty minutes or else

pollution problems may be caused by that which remains uneaten and falls to the pool floor.

Autumn and winter Waterlilies and other deep water aquatics can be allowed to die back naturally in the autumn, but other aquatics need to be tidied up in the same way as herbaceous plants. As soon as marginal subjects have finished flowering, remove all the dead and dying foliage, being careful not to cut hollow-stemmed varieties beneath water level. Even though adapted for an aquatic environment, such plants will die if their stems become filled with water.

Most of the free-floating aquatics disappear for the winter, forming turions or winter buds which drop to the floor of the pool. They re-appear in spring when the water is gently warmed by the sun. Because algae can rapidly invade the pool during the first sunny days of spring, it is useful to remove some of the turions before they fall to the floor of the pool and place them in a jar of water with a layer of soil in the bottom. If kept in a frost-free place they can be brought out into the warmth during early spring and encouraged into growth. They will then be of a reasonable size to shade the water in the pool when the algae first invade.

Most popular coldwater fish can tolerate our winters without too much trouble. The prudent fish keeper, however, will ensure their good health before they undertake their enforced torpor, by feeding liberally with high protein foods such as daphnia and dried flies in the early autumn.

Provided there is a minimum depth of at least 45cm (18in) at one point in the pool most fish will survive unaided. That is unless icing is prolonged. It is not intense cold that causes problems, but the trapping of noxious gases by the ice which, in turn, asphyxiate the fish.

If a fountain is used in the pool during the summer, then a pool heater can be connected in its place for the winter months. This is very economical to run and consists of a brass rod containing a heating element attached to a small polystyrene float.

Alternatively, a hole can be maintained in the ice by standing a pan of boiling water on the surface and allowing it to melt through. This is a long and tedious process, but is infinitely preferable to hitting the ice with a blunt instrument in the hope of making a hole. The shock waves created by such methods may kill or concuss the fish.

SIXTY OF THE BEST

Several types of plant need to be used in combination if the gardener is to achieve a good visual effect from the pool as well as create the all-important natural balance in the watery environment. Under water-lilies and deep water aquatics the figures given refer to the depths of water at which each cultivar may be successfully grown. Other figures refer to plant height.

Hemerocallis **'Torpoint'**

WATERLILIES – *NYMPHAEA*

'Froebeli'. Deep blood-red flowers with orange stamens and dull purplish leaves. Free-flowering. 45-60cm (18-24in).

'Gonnere'. Double pure white globular flowers with conspicuous green sepals. Luxuriant pea-green leaves. Sometimes sold as 'Crystal White'. 45-75cm (18-30in).

'Graziella'. Orange-red flowers which age to red. Olive-green leaves blotched with purple and brown. 30-60cm (12 to 24in).

'James Brydon'. Large crimson paeony-shaped blossoms float amongst dark purplish-green leaves which are often flecked with maroon. 45-90cm (18-36in).

laydekeri
'Fulgens'. Fragrant bright crimson flowers with reddish stamens. Dark green leaves with purplish undersides. 30-60cm (12-24in).

laydekeri
'Purpurata'. Rich vinous-red blooms borne in profusion amongst small dark green leaves with purplish undersides. 30-60cm (12-24in).

marliacea **'Chromatella'**

marliacea
'Albida'. Large white fragrant blossoms with golden centres. The sepals and backs of the petals are often flushed with soft pink. Deep green leaves with purplish undersides. 45-90cm (18-36in).

marliacea
'Carnea'. A strong growing flesh-pink cultivar which is often called 'Morning Glory'. Flowers on newly established plants are often white for the first few months. Vanilla scented. 45cm-1.5m (1½-5ft).

marliacea **'Carnea'**

marliacea
'Chromatella'. An old and popular cultivar. Large soft-yellow flowers are produced amongst handsome mottled foliage. 45-75cm (18-30in).

'Gonnere'

'Mrs. Richmond'. Beautiful pale rose-pink flowers which pass to crimson with age. Conspicuous golden stamens. Plain green leaves. 45-75cm (18-30in).

odorata minor
A splendid miniature variety with fragrant star-shaped flowers and soft green leaves. Ideal for tubs, sinks and for very shallow pools. 30cm (12in).

'Mrs. Richmond'

pygmaea 'Alba'

'Rose Arey'

odorata
'Sulphurea'. A popular canary-yellow cultivar with dark green heavily mottled foliage. Flowers star-shaped and slightly fragrant. 45-60cm (18-24in).

pygmaea
'Alba'. The tiniest white variety available. Small dark green leaves. 30cm (12in).

pygmaea
'Helvola'. Beautiful canary-yellow flowers with orange stamens are produced continuously throughout the summer. Olive-green foliage heavily mottled with purple and brown. 30cm (12in).

'Rose Arey' Large open stellate flowers that have a central boss of golden stamens and an almost over-powering aniseed fragrance. 45-75cm (18-30in).

DEEP WATER AQUATICS

Aponogeton distachyus
Water hawthorn. One of the most versatile aquatics that the gardener can grow. Small, more or less oblong, green floating leaves and pure white forked blossoms with distinctive black stamens. Strongly scented of vanilla. Spring and summer. 30-90cm (1 to 3ft).

Nymphoides peltata
Water fringe. Known by generations of gardeners as *Villarsia nymphoides,* this is a small lily-like aquatic with tiny rounded green leaves and delicately fringed yellow blossoms. Summer. 30-75cm (12-30in).

Orontium aquaticum
Golden club. Grown by some gardeners as a marginal plant, this splendid little character is most adaptable. It has handsome lance-shaped glaucous floating foliage and erect spikes of gold and white flowers held just above the surface of the water. Late spring and early summer. 30-75cm (12-30in).

FLOATING PLANTS

Azolla caroliniana
Fairy moss. This little member of the fern family has coarse green floating fronds. When young, or growing in shade, they are green, but at the approach of winter or in full sun they turn red.

Hydrocharis morsus-ranae
Frogbit. This looks rather like a small waterlily, having tiny kidney-shaped floating leaves in neat floating rosettes. The flowers are three-petalled and produced during the summer months.

Stratiotes aloides
Water soldier. Large spiky rosettes of bronze-green foliage very much like a pineapple top. Papery white or pinkish blossoms are produced during late summer. *Stratiotes* reproduces freely from runners. Young individuals can be detached and will form a new colony of plants.

Trapa natans
Water chestnut. Rosettes of dark green rhomboidal leaves support creamy-white axillary flowers. Botanically this plant is an annual as it grows afresh each year from spiny nuts. These fall to the floor of the pool each autumn in ever increasing numbers, germinating and returning to the surface during late spring. Most gardeners gather a few nuts during early autumn and keep them in a jar of water with a little soil in the bottom in a frost-free place, or else wrapped in damp sphagnum. This enables them to be started into growth earlier and assists in the annual battle against the appearance of early summer algae.

Orontium aquaticum

SUBMERGED OXYGENATING PLANTS

Ceratophyllum demersum
Hornwort, coontail. An excellent plant for difficult cool shady places. Dense whorls of very narrow, dark green bristly foliage which form a resting winter bud.

Elodea canadensis
Anacharis, Canadian pondweed. A vigorous, but excellent submerged plant which sometimes needs controlling in large expanses of water. In the garden pool it seldom creates a problem. Dense bushy stems with whorls of dark green leaves.

Hottonia palustris
Water violet. Large whorls of lime-green divided foliage support bold erect spikes of lilac or white blossoms during early summer.

Lagarosiphon major
Goldfish weed. Also known as *Elodea crispa,* this is probably the most widely grown submerged aquatic of all. It is this dark green crispy-leaved plant that is sold in large numbers by pet shops for goldfish bowls. Apart from being an efficient functional plant it is more or less evergreen, thus enabling growth to start more rapidly and effectively in the spring when algae-laden water is more likely.

Myriophyllum spicatum
Spiked milfoil. Small crimson flowers are borne on the ends of soft, feathery grey-green foliage. A first class spawning medium for the goldfish breeder.

Potamogeton crispus
Curled pondweed. Handsome foliage like a bronze-green seaweed. Translucent, with crinkled edges and supporting short spikes of relatively insignificant crimson and cream flowers.

Ranunculus aquatilis
Water crowfoot. Deeply dissected submerged foliage and clover-like floating leaves which give rise to tiny pure gold and white blossoms during early summer. The common name alludes to the habit of the underwater foliage which looks very much like an outstretched bird's foot – hence its name.

MARGINAL PLANTS

Acorus calamus
Sweet flag. A leafy green iris-like plant. The variegated cultivar 'Variegatus' has foliage that is streaked with cream and rose. 45-75cm (18-30in).

***Acorus calamus* 'Variegatus'**

Butomus umbellatus
Flowering rush. Umbels of rose-pink blossoms amongst curious twisted, three-sided rush-like foliage. Late summer. 45-90cm (18-36in).

Calla palustris
Bog arum. A small scrambling plant like a dwarf arum lily. Pure white spathes followed by succulent red berries. Spring. 23-30cm (8-12in).

***Caltha palustris* 'Flore-pleno'**

Cyperus longus

Caltha palustris
Marsh marigold, kingcup. Bright golden blossoms during early spring above handsome dark green foliage. *Caltha p.*'Alba' is white and the cultivar 'Flore- pleno' has fully double golden yellow flowers.
Spring. 30-75cm (12-30in).

***Glyceria aquatica* 'Variegata'**

Cyperus longus
Sweet galingale. A hardy version of the popular indoor umbrella plant *Cyperus alternifolius*. Stiff terminal umbels of spiky leaves which radiate from the stem like the ribs of an umbrella. Excellent for colonising wet soil at the poolside.

Eriophorum angustifolium
Cotton grass. Although there are a number of different species of *Eriophorum* around, it is only this one that is commonly cultivated. Characteristic of boggy moorland, it is an acid-loving plant with grassy leaves and distinctive cotton wool-like seeding heads. Summer. 30-60cm (12-24in).

Glyceria aquatica
'Variegata'. Variegated water grass. Cream and green-striped leaves suffused with rose-pink during early spring. 75-90cm (30-36in).

Iris laevigata
A lovely blue aquatic iris which has given rise to many splendid cultivars. 'Snowdrift' is pure white, 'Colchesteri' purple and white, while 'Rose Queen' is a delicate shade of pink. Summer. 60cm (24in).

Juncus effusus
'Spiralis'. A twisted rush which is interesting rather than beautiful. The dark green stems resemble a Harry Lauder walking stick. 45cm (18in).

Lysichitum americanum
American skunk cabbage. Large yellow arum-like flowers are produced during April before any foliage appears. It is from the huge cabbagy leaves that the plant derives its common name. A slightly more modest species, *L.camschatcense* has white spathes. 90cm-1.2m (3-4ft).

Mentha aquatica
Water mint. A strongly aromatic creeping aquatic version of the common garden mint. Downy leaves with a purplish cast and whorls of lilac-pink flowers. Late summer. 35-45cm (14-18in).

Menyanthes trifoliata
Bog bean. White, finely fringed flowers and dark green foliage like that of a broad bean. Late spring. 30cm (12in)

Myosotis scorpioides
Water forget-me-not. Similar to our familiar spring flowering forget-me-not, but a reliable perennial. The cultivar 'Semperflorens' is even finer. Late spring and early summer. 23-30cm (9-12in).

Pontederia cordata
Pickerel. A splendid late summer flowering aquatic with handsome glossy green foliage and spikes of soft blue flowers. 60-90cm (24-36in).

Sagittaria japonica
Arrowhead. Bright green arrow-shaped foliage and spikes of white flowers. The double form 'Plena' has blossoms like tiny powder puffs. Summer. 60cm (24in).

Scirpus lacustris
Bulrush. Dark green spiky stems and tassels of brownish flowers. 'Albescens' has stems of sulphurous white, while the zebra rush, S. 'Zebrinus' is alternately barred with cream and green. 60-90cm (24-36in).

Menyanthes trifoliata

***Juncus effusus* 'Spiralis'**

Pontederia cordata

Typha angustifolia
Reedmace. Popularly but erroneously known as the bulrush. Slender blue-green leaves and thick brown poker-like heads. A species known as *T.laxmannii* is of more modest proportions, (60cm-1.2m/2-4ft), and the grassy leaved *T.minima* is a complete dwarf. (30cm/12in). Late summer.

Veronica beccabunga
Brooklime. The only truly aquatic member of this popular genus of garden plants. Evergreen scrambling foliage that is excellent for disguising the harsh pool edge. Sparkling tiny blue flowers. Summer. 15-30cm (6-12in).

BOG GARDEN PLANTS

Astilbe arendsii
Formerly known as spiraea, this group of hybrids includes many good, named cultivars in a wide range of colours. They have spires of frothy flowers above compact deeply cut foliage. 'Red Sentinel', 'Rose Perle' and the dwarf white 'Irrlicht' are all good cultivars. Summer. 60-90cm (24-36in).

Cardamine pratensis
Cuckoo flower. A charming spring flowering waterside plant with single lilac-rose blossoms and hummocks of pale green fern-like foliage. Its double form, *flore-pleno*, is even more lovely. 30cm (12in).

Astilbe arendsii

Cardamine pratensis flore-pleno

Gunnera manicata
Only for the larger bog garden, these impressive rhubarb-like plants attain sizeable proportions. Their rootstock appears as a huge scaly lump which requires the protection of discarded leaves or straw for the winter. The immense bristly inflorescence is like an enormous bottle brush. A most imposing plant when sufficient room is available. 2-2.5m (6½ – 8ft).

Hemerocallis Hybrids
Daylily. All the named cultivars of hemerocallis prefer constant moisture, even though they survive under dry border conditions. There are innumerable named varieties of these lovely perennials, including 'Golden Chimes', 'Pink Charm', and the bright orange 'Margaret Perry'. Daylilies produce trumpet or funnel-shaped blossoms that individually last a single day, but so many are produced that there is a continuous show throughout the summer. 30-90cm (12-36in).

***Hemerocallis* 'Burning Daylight'**

Hosta fortunei
Gardeners with plenty of room should grow this majestic large-leaved plantain lily. Apart from its beautifully sculptured pale green leaves it delights the water gardener with bold spikes of handsome lilac funnel-shaped blossoms. Summer. 30-45cm (12-18in).

***Hosta fortunei* 'Aurea'**

Primula florindae

Iris kaempferi
Japanese clematis-flowered iris. Strong tufts of broad grassy foliage support large brightly coloured clematis-like blossoms. There are many named varieties, but the mixed Higo strain produce the most spectacular flowers. Must have acid soil. Summer. 60-75cm (24-30in).

Iris sibirica
Siberian iris. Easily grown iris with clumps of grassy foliage and less spectacular, but equally attractive flowers. Not fussy about soil conditions and will flourish in both wet and slightly damp conditions. There are many cultivars, but 'Perry's Blue' is the best known. Summer. 60-75cm (24-30in).

Lobelia fulgens
A perennial lobelia with lance-shaped foliage of the most intense and lovely beetroot-red topped with spires of vivid scarlet flowers. Hybrids derived from this and the slightly tender *L.cardinalis* include 'Queen Victoria' red, 'Huntsman' scarlet and 'Mrs Humbert' flesh pink. Summer. 60-90cm (24-36in).

Lythrum salicaria
Purple loosestrife. Many gardeners will know of our native purple loosestrife with its bold spires of rich rose-purple blossoms. But there are much improved garden varieties that add colour and zest to the bog garden. 'The Beacon' is purple, 'Lady Sackville' rose-pink, and 'Robert' soft pink. All flower from mid to late summer. 75cm-1m (30-40in).

Peltiphyllum peltatum
Umbrella plant. Surprisingly a close relative of the saxifrages, this marvellous bog plant produces dense pink heads of tiny pink flowers on stout stems during early spring before any foliage appears. The succeeding leaves are large rounded and umbrella-like, of a bronze-green hue, and held aloft on bold central leaf stalks. 90cm-1.2m (3 to 4ft).

Primula
There are endless primulas that can be grown under bog garden conditions. These comprise most of the late spring and summer flowering candelabra species and hybrids. These include the red *Primula japonica* (60cm/24in) and *P.pulverulenta* (75cm/30in), the orange *P.chungensis* (30cm/12in) as well as the rosy-purple *P.beesiana* (60cm/24in) and yellow *P.helodoxa* (90cm/36in). Other kinds of primula that do well are the early spring flowered drumstick primula, *P.denticulata* (30-45cm/12-18in), the cowslip-like *P.florindae* (90cm/36in) and tiny ground-hugging *P.rosea* (15cm/6in).

Rheum palmatum
Ornamental rhubarb. This is one of the most inspiring of the decorative rhubarbs with broad spreading foliage and spikes of creamy-white flowers almost 2m (6½ft) high. The variety *tanguticum* has divided foliage and crimson blossoms, while 'Bowles Crimson' has leaves with a deep purplish-red suffusion. 90cm-1.2m (3-4ft).

Trollius europaeus
Globe flower. Buttercup-like plants with globular blossoms in shades of orange, cream and yellow. The foliage is large, dark green, and similar to the common buttercup, making a neat basal hummock from which arise wiry stems bearing the rounded waxy flowers. There are many named kinds, but 'Orange Crest' and 'Golden Queen' are amongst the best. Late spring and early summer. 75cm (30in).

INDEX AND ACKNOWLEDGEMENTS

algae, 6, 7, 21, 23, 33-4
Alisma plantago-aquatica, 26
Aponogeton distachyus, **21**, 26

bog plants, 25, 45-47

caddis flies, 35
carp, 29, **29**
cascades, 18-19
catfish, 31, **31**
cats, 34
concrete pools, 14-15, **15**

depth of pools, 9
design, 8-9
dirty water, 34
diseases, 33
duckweed, **33**

filters, 19
fish, 22, 23, 24
  choosing, 28
  diseases, 35
  raising, 29-30
floating plants, 24, 41
formal pools, 8, **9**
fountains, 8, 16-19, **16, 17**
frogs, 32, **32**

glass fibre, pools, 12-13, **13**
  waterfalls, 19
goldfish, 7, 12, 28-9, **28, 29**

Hemerocallis 'Pink Prelude', **25**
herons, 34

illusions, 7
informal pools, 8, **9**
Iris, 27
  laevigata 'Variegata', 25

leaves, 7
light, 21
lime, 15
liners, 10-12, **11**
  installation, 11
  polythene, 10
  PVC, 10
  rubber, 10
  size, 10-11

marginal plants, 25, 42-5
marsh marigolds, 27
Menyanthes trifoliata, 26
mussels, freshwater, 32
Myosotis scorpioides, 26

natural water, 8-9
newts, 32
Nymphaea, 39-40
  pygmaea 'Alba', 26
  see also waterlilies
orfe, 29, **29**
oxygenating plants, 21, 24, 42

planting baskets, 6, 9, 21, 23, **25**
plants, 20-5
  bog, 25, 45-7
  choosing, 22
  deep water, 23-4, 41
  depth of water, 9
  floating, 24, 41
  formal pools, 8
  fountains and, 16
  informal pools, 8
  marginal, 25, 43-5
  oxygenating 21, 24, 42
  propagation, 26-7, **27**
polythene liners, 10
Pontederia cordata, 26
pools, concrete, 14-15, **15**
  construction, 10-15, **11, 13, 15**
  depth, 9
  design, 8-9
  filters, 19
  formal, 8, **9**
  glass fibre, 12-13, **13**
  informal, 8, **9**
  liners, 10-12
  natural water, 9
  rock, 12
  siting, 6-7
  water condition, 33-4
propagation, 26-7, **27**
  by division, 27
  from cuttings, 26
  from eyes, 26
  from seed, 26
pumps, 16-17
PVC liners, 10

rock pools, 12
rubber liners, 10

sealants, 15
seed, 26
shelter, 6, 7
siting pools, 6-7
snails, water, 30-1
soil, 23, 26
sunlight, 6, 7, 10

tench, 31, **31**
toads, 32
trees, 7
Veronica beccabunga, 26

water, dirty, 34
  green, 33-4
waterfalls, 16-19, **18, 19**
waterlilies, 9, 16, **18, 22-3**, 23-4, 39-40
  propagation, 26, **27**
waterlily aphid, 35
waterlily leaf spot, 35
waterlily root rot, 35
wind, 6

Picture credits

Ray Duns: 21(t)
Lyn and Derek Gould: 1,9(t),16,18(b),19,21(b),23,25(t),28,29(bl,br), 32(bl,br),36/7,39(t),41,43(b),45(tr),46(t)
Bill Howes: 31(bl,br)
Harry Smith Horticultural Photographic Collection: 4/5,6,7,9(r),17(t,b), 18(t),20,22,22/3,24,25(b),33,38,39(bl,br),40(tl,tr,bl),42,43(tl,tr), 44(t,b),45(l,br),46(bl,br)

Artwork by Richard Prideaux and Steve Sandilands